Bittersweet *Love* Poems

Linda Amos

ISBN: Paperback 979-8-9912637-0-2
ISBN: Ebook 979-8-9912637-1-9

Design and publishing assistance by The Happy Self-Publisher.

Linda Amos Books, LLC

Cover illustration by T. Angela
Author photo by Earle Brown − Eyes of Distinction

*To the man who inspired most of
my bittersweet love poems*

Contents

My Bittersweet Love Poems

My love poems capture feelings of happiness and pain
as I think about those same moments again.
They tell you of change, predicaments, and life.
But most of all, they tell you of love and its strife.

When love, to me, has seemed beautiful and warm,
I've usually been unable to write a poem.
The same thing applies to life and friends.
Don't get the impression that bitterness only ascends

to haunt the life of one particular girl,
for she's found moments of peace in this world.
My love poems aren't meant to be beautiful or memorable,
nor are they meant to make you feel comfortable.

After reading my love poems, if you disagree,
just remember that I only expound on what appears to me.

Ever So Perfect

He's her strong foundation,
her only source of elation,
nature's number one creation,
the strength of a nation.

The opposite of dissipation
and slow degradation,
he refuses to be the cause of negation,
for he's indeed a masculine sensation.

There is, however, one complication:
he's strictly a figment of her imagination.

Take Me There

I want to go
where I'll never see snow,
where birds always sing,
and phones of good luck always ring.

I want to see
photos of you and me
having a marvelous time,
because everything was simple and fine.

Please let me hear
you say that I'm so dear
to your heart
and that we'll never part.

Just take me in your arms, and I'll go, see, and hear
all of this, every day of the year.

Greetings

Say hello
to the radiant glow
of the successes and promises of tomorrow.

Say goodbye
to the futile try
of unhappy days gone by.

The jeans-clad, cool jiver
has been converted to a survivor.
That's why
he's said goodbye

to the heartache, disaster, and pain
of the thunderous, murderous rain,
and is planning to say hello
as tomorrow's acclaimed hero.

Yes, you and I
must definitely give it a try.

That Special Someone

You came into my life like a leaf borne on the wind;
you gave me the immeasurable happiness only you could bring.
A special kind of love developed; we couldn't be torn apart,
for we had become inseparable. In other words, you'd touched my heart.

And forever this is the way it'll be
because our love will last eternally.
Keep this in mind no matter what you do:
you're mine, and I'll always love you.

Silence

I hear the sounds, the shouts, the words
as the silent plea of a heartbroken girl.
I feel the love, the disunity, the life
like the silent plea of a deserted wife.

I smell the perfume, the garbage, the rain-splattered dirt
as the silent plea of an unbearable hurt.
I taste the spicy, the sour, the sweet
like the silent plea an unwanted lover must greet.

I touch the silky, the satin, the rough
and feel the silent plea of one who has had enough.
I sense the silence no one else perceives
because I'm the one who aches and grieves.

Love Is Bittersweet

When I'm happy, some fault of yours
mars the tranquility that's been a part of my soul.
Sometimes when I'm sad, your warm love comforts me—
you make me forget that pain ever existed in my life.

We're sometimes strangers to one another.
You won't show your feelings,
and I won't expose mine.

We need to get together and find the weaknesses
of our little love affair.
I'd hate to lose you because you're so unique.

There's no one else who'll receive all that's possible,
give all that's possible,
and still have enough left to share with others.
Oh, well, that's the bittersweet aura of love.

My Love

You gave me one command
that I couldn't quite understand.
That command was that I not fall in love with you.
Right now, I can't deny that my love is true.

What could be so wrong with letting my feelings flow free?
In the beginning, that was the way it was meant to be.
As I look back over our relationship, I see changes you've made—
changes in your shrewd tactics and the game you play.

Why couldn't you continue to cuddle me and call me your cat-eyed
doll baby
and let me go on thinking that love was a maybe?
I can deal with the situation maturely. In case I don't,
I'll walk away from you because that's what I would want.

If you ever feel my love for you has reached a dead-end street
or become a disheartening game in which our eyes can't meet
for fear of what's trapped inside,
be honest with me and don't try to hide.

Our relationship is something we'll eventually have to face,
So don't think of it as a disgrace.
Think of it as my forbidden fruit put in its respective place.
I'm not asking you for love or another chance.
I'm just asking you to try to face the realities of romance.

To the Man I Used to Love

I know what your problem is, and I'm sorry to say
that it'll be a long time before it goes away.
You think you're a big man, too old to be a boy,
and yet you're too young to play with a man's toy.

You think a boy is a man only after he's had sex,
but I'm going to tell you that you're incorrect.
It takes much more to make a boy a man,
and I want you to find out what it is if you can.

Add both physical and mental maturity to a lot of common sense,
or you'll cause a lot of problems at someone else's expense.
The next time you proclaim yourself a man, remember what I'm saying.
Don't try to grow up so fast; instead, start listening and obeying.

You'll have sufficient time for life's forbidden pleasures.
You'll have enough time for success' valuable treasures.
Slow down a little and enjoy life while you can.
Don't follow your friends; you'll shorten your lifespan.

You aren't experiencing heartache right now,
but one day you will, and Wow!
You'll look back on the ease of yesterday
and wonder why the happiness had to go away.

Friend, Lover, Enemy

You've been my friend,
my lover, and my enemy without end.
Somehow, I forget everything you've been
except my lover, again and again.

From the second week I knew you
I had loved you so much, I didn't know what to do.
Therefore, I've let our love run its course.
That's why our relationship has always been a source

of laughter, pain, passion, and fun.
That's why you once again have to run
away and hide from my love's high-intensity beam.
No one, not even you, can rip my love's seam.

Love's Lilting Language

I love you enough to die for you today, tomorrow, even yesterday,
but if you don't love me, then what more can I say?
For five long years, I've waited patiently, with loss of pride
simply because you couldn't commit to having a wife by your side.

Somehow being your wife is secondary to my being the love of your life,
and that's the reason why I don't mind my present strife.
My darling, please don't be afraid of my love for you,
for I know that I'll never stop loving you no matter what you do.

A Case of Love

I was a lonely girl bewildered by love
when you came into my life like an undeveloped dove.
I gave you pleasure with unnatural ease,
but it was nothing compared to moments like these.

We were separated for months on hand,
and our relationship I began to understand.
The mystery of true love I slowly unraveled.
The road of heartache I often traveled.

Before that, I had a secret love affair
while another man loved me, but I didn't care.
My secret lover just pushed me aside—
my love for him was impossible to hide.

I was running away from this kind of pain
when my sunshine appeared through the rain.
You're the man of whom I speak.
You're the relief I had come to seek.

I fell in love head over heel.
Your love for me seemed oh, so real.
I knew that something was sadly wrong
when you seemed like a singer without a song.

Suddenly I found myself thrust into despair,
for you had no reason to even want to care.
You told me things I know aren't true.
I never expected to hear them from you.

I thought you were mature enough to understand
the differences between a boy and a man.
I see now that you never really cared
about any of the experiences you and I shared.

I've used this little time to really think it through,
and I've come to the conclusion that I don't need you.
You were a little too quick to believe that lie
and a little too quick to say goodbye.

Before I crumble, before I swoon,
I'll tell you that you made your move too soon.

I Wanted to Love You

I wanted to love you, but you pushed me aside.
I wanted to help you, but you preferred to hide.
I wanted to hold you, but you said it was too late.
I wanted to smile, but my tears wouldn't abate.

I wanted to sing to you, but you covered your ears.
I wanted to tell you a story, but it intensified your fears.
I wanted to dance for you, but the steps weren't right.
I wanted to see you, but there was no light.

I wanted to build your life, but you tore it down.
I wanted to make you a king, but you destroyed the crown.
I wanted to light your fire, but you blew it out.
I wanted to scream, but I could only shout.

I wanted to expel the cold and keep you warm.
I decided to write you a beautiful poem—
a poem of love, peace, and eternity.
A poem exclusively for you, from me.

A poem as tranquil as a sleeping dove.
Our poem of bittersweet, tragic love.

Rebuilding Love

I made a plan, and I based it on love,
a product of togetherness with intervention from above.
I added to my foundation all that I could perceive.
I gave you everything you could ever want to receive.

I only held back true love because I somehow feared
that one day when I loved you, my heart would be seared.
After our time had passed, I cared for many more,
but it always resulted in someone beating my score.

In two of these affairs, my heart knew no relief.
The guys I cared for caused me nothing but grief.
I had to give them up and go my own sweet way
for they loved other women, and this was the price I had to pay.

I rekindled a dying fire and came back to you
to rediscover every beautiful moment that we had survived through.
Our infatuation developed into love that knew no earthly bounds.
We conquered the unconquerable and tread on sacred grounds.

Now, as our love grows stronger, we leave behind the past,
for we have the kind of love that I know will always last.

A Bittersweet Love Affair

Before I knew you as a sweetheart, I knew you as a friend—
a friend of the opposite sex whose admiration was without end.
And once, when I was lonely, you told me a few of your views.
You wanted to get to know me better, but I knew it was no use.

I couldn't communicate with you at that time.
We were worlds apart—your views too different from mine.
You introduced me to a friend of yours.
To turn him away was several difficult chores.

One day, I made you angry and soothed you with a kiss.
After that, everything seemed to be a little amiss.
You used to put your arm around me and we would take a walk.
When you saw a friend of yours, you and she would begin to talk.

I went my lonely way and left you alone
for a while at least, but I failed to overcome
my urge to love someone else's man
and that's when our havoc began.

You told me that I was all you needed—
in that respect, I had succeeded.
But for some strange reason, I didn't believe you.
I didn't think you would help me make it through.

I fell deeply in love with another guy.
I don't really know the reason why.
To get him off my mind and free from my heart
took a lot of time and courage on my part.

I finally succeeded in letting him go.
The pain caused, no one will ever know.
I became involved with the guy who helped me forget him.
Because of this man, our future remained dim.

I wanted both of you, but I wanted him much more
because he gave me a stronger relationship and a much higher score.
For a very simple reason, he and I were parted.
This left me disillusioned and brokenhearted.

I started going with you on the rebound
and rekindled the fire that we had once found.
I felt that you weren't giving me enough tender loving care,
so I began yet another carefree love affair.

I divided my attention between you two.
He called me a fool for continuing to love you
because you didn't really want me, just all you could get.
Part of that was my fault and that's what I regret.

I failed to notice your hurt and the pain in your eyes,
and that's how you caught me by surprise.
We decided to start all over again
with the hope that we would definitely win.

I thought you could trust me, but I made my third mistake
with the player type of guy who is as sneaky as a snake.
He's the cause of the misunderstanding between us—
a subject that is still too touchy for you to discuss.

He lied to you about me and gave you the impression
I'm the type of woman unworthy of your possession.
He covered up the truth with some of his sweet, well-conceived lies
that explained the *hows* but mystified the *whys*.

Each time you heard one, you looked at me with disgust,
but never would you explain the rift between us.
I know you think I'm a woman with whom you have no chance,
but you must understand I'm an unfortunate victim of circumstance.

I can do anything and be anything you want me to
simply because I deeply love you.

My Desolation

It's hard for me to leave you behind,
but harder to get you off my mind.
It could be so simple if I wanted it to be.
The simplicity depends entirely on me.

Even though love isn't something you know,
I just don't want to let you go,
For love isn't all I want in life.
I need the pain, heartache, and strife.

Love will make up twenty times over
for all the desolation I'll uncover.
The thing that causes it to hurt so bad
is that you're someone I never really had.

One of these days I'll get my due
Because one of these days I *will* have you.

We're the Past

My heart's filled with memories, those remnants of you and me,
as I think of us, my dear, and the way things ought to be.
I remember all of the heartaches and all of the warm embraces

that I have experienced because of you, the love of my life.
I remember all of the strife
that has been an integral part
of the breaking of my heart.

I wouldn't say that it's your fault, but neither is it mine.
It just happens to be both of ours combined.
It began a long time ago, way back in the past.
I didn't know it would happen or that our affair wouldn't last,
but now I've decided to consider it the past.

Startled

I went to the edge of reality and began to perceive
a man willing to give, a man ready to receive.
I thought he was giving me all there was to give.
I thought I was living the best I could live.

It took me a long time to see that I was getting only a part,
for his main woman had his heart.
When I first learned of his main woman, I knew of someone else
and thought there was nobody but her and myself.

I was shocked to find that we weren't the only ones on his list,
And soon after that, I alone was dismissed.
Startled, I had to learn the hard way
that the man I deeply loved would be swift to say

I mean nothing to him. He won't let me mess up his "good thang."
And until he changes, some expect me to hang
on in there for the longest,
for they think I'm strongest

when it comes to the man who had my love,
that Romeo who evades me like a dove.

An Outsider Told Me

Your friends think you're lying, and I'll tell you why.
You never tell men you love them, and never tell them goodbye.
Men assume that you're theirs without a good reason.
When men walk out on you, you show no signs of grieving.

You tell men to love other women, and the men just don't understand
that you're only a little girl trying to love a big man.
You even have men thinking that you're trying to play the field,
but the men just don't know that your feelings are real.

Slow down a bit and take life a stride at a time,
and stop pretending to love a man who should be mine.
Then a good man will be able to keep up with you,
and I'm sure he'll see you through.

A man respects a woman like you, with lots of scruples and morals.
Some will think you have no taste, that you are a man borrower,
But they wouldn't even think so
if they really got to know

the true depth of the feelings you possess
and the basis of your source of happiness.
As I depart from you today, I leave this message behind:
find the man you love, and love the man you find.

What It Takes

If every dream I dreamed came true,
if my every moment was spent with you,
if desire itself could be quenched totally,
if I could be happy eternally,

if people could understand I have to be me,
then I could feel totally free.

Freedom

The day will come when I'll be free,
then you won't have to worry about me.
I'll have time to do what I please,
and I won't beg you on bent knees.

I won't obey you blindly anymore.
This little girl will gladly let you go.
I was filled with dread before I met you.
I was afraid and didn't know what to do.

I was hurt because I loved another woman's man.
When he tired of me, he turned and ran.
This episode made me realize
some men are full of deceit and lies.

When you came into my life, I thought you were different,
but I was in for a big disappointment.
You and I had a lot in common,
and it took all of the courage I could summon

to turn away and let you travel your lonely road,
knowing that you carried a heavy load.
I'll never be happy until I let you go.
I'll never be free until I let you know

of the exact way that I feel.
You must know that my love is real.

It Wasn't Meant to Be

I wasn't playing hard to get or anything of that sort.
Loving someone else's man was simply a last resort.
I couldn't turn around and erase my tracks,
for I had stabbed too many people in their backs.

My man turned away and left me alone.
I had only his memories when he was gone.
This man meant so much to me.
I guess our love wasn't meant to be.

How can I describe the way he made me feel?
How could I believe his love was real?

You Didn't Belong in My Life

She couldn't do for you what I was doing.
She kept you on the run, always pursuing.
I gave you what she could never give.
I gave you a true reason to want to live.

I gave you love that would last.
I gave you a reason to forget the past.
Our relationship was doomed to an early death
that proceeded with such precision and stealth.

There were many things I couldn't understand
because, unconsciously, I loved another woman's man.
You wanted to keep me from feeling any pain,
but this would have resulted in no one's gain.

You're still important at this time,
but you never belonged in this life of mine.

I'm Sorry

I'm sorry we met in the wrong place.
I'm sorry we started our relationship the wrong way.
I'm sorry I was a little too easy.
I'm sorry we parted for a stupid reason.

I'm sorry we found one another at the wrong time.
I'm sorry you blew this mind of mine.
I'm sorry you turned me on with sweet kisses and affection.
I'm sorry I responded to an imperfect connection.

I'm sorry you put me down so cold.
I'm sorry you didn't realize that my love had grown old.
I'm sorry I didn't fully recognize you for what you are.
I'm sorry I have to love you from afar.

I'm sorry that you have me feeling so blue,
but most of all *I'm sorry* I fell in love with you.

Remember Me

When you've run away from the past so bleak,
when you've found the woman that you now seek,
when you've made a fortune and your mind's at ease,
when you've forgotten your elders' criticisms and pleas,

when your wife and children leave your side,
when there seems to be no place where you can hide,
when your hair is gray and your steps are slow,
when sweet pain relief you can't know,

when your hands tremble for every move you make,
when your body racks for every breath you take,
when your insides seem to be churning away,
when you don't know the difference between night and day,

remember me and the price you'll have to pay.

Remember the girl whose love was so deep.
Remember when you treated her like a creep.
Remember the girl whose consideration was without end.
Remember when you called her everything but your friend.

Remember the boy she thought she could trust.
Remember the situation between us.
Remember the reason you believed that lie.
Remember the time you made me cry.

When the time has come for your taste of eternity,
Please, please just *remember me*.

If Today Be Sweet

On a hot summer's day in July,
for some reason (I don't know exactly why)
I committed the most regretful crime
of doing you wrong in that little time.

Just the feel of your strong, gentle arms
made me do what others consider wrong.
We shared only a few, short days
in which there was no time for delays.

It seemed as if we knew we would be parted,
but we just couldn't end what we had started.
Our relationship had to come to a close,
and I am the only one who knows

that all I have of you are your memories—
those sweet reminders of our hours of ease.
In trying to get you off my mind,
I realize the past is hard to leave behind.

When I tried, I almost fell.
Then someone else caused me to rebel
against the old custom and the ancient way
of spending many and many a lonely day

grieving to hear you say, "You're mine tomorrow. You were mine
yesterday,
but most of all, you're mine today."
I know I didn't give you the chance to love me
or the love in my heart. (That would have caused you to hurt me.)

So I forgot about you and laid down my big plan
of having you forever as my main man.
I became involved with someone else
who would really need me and love me for myself.

In this affair, I was the one to play the fool
by thinking what I did was suave and cool.
Right then, I meant the things I said,
knowing nothing of the trouble I bred.

Excluding the havoc we had wrought,
everything between us had come to a halt.
Nothing you can do can change the way I feel.
The things people say can't make us seem unreal.

None of this matters, not even heartache and deceit,
for I have no time for another love if today be sweet.

The Agony of Deceit

Once upon a time, a few heartbreaks ago,
a man taught me everything about love I needed to know.
He gave me a different name, and I considered him a player.
He and I had an understanding, for neither of us was a betrayer

until the time came when we could no longer communicate.
It was during this time that I anticipated heartache.
To avert the pain and stagnation of being brokenhearted,
I began to cheat on him and we didn't become parted.

I knew we would never make it if he made a fool of me,
so I decided to cheat and thereby remain free.
I'm sorry I can't tell him of my part-time love,
a love who's always been as unreachable as a headstrong dove.

I hope not to fall deeper in love by going about it this way
because I know from the past that love's pain will always stay.
I wanted him and me to be true so very bad;
I wanted us to be happy together, not sad.

I let some of my wishes fly and played a different game
knowing that the outcome would always be the same.
I know he thinks I don't love him because I played around
but I'm very much satisfied with the kind of love I've found.

As I cheat on him and as he cheats on me,
I hope we'll remain in love forever—an eternity.

The Irony of Two

First there was one who didn't want her initially.
Then there were none that anyone else could see.
Next came a man who liked her a lot,
but she ignored him because he didn't make her instantly hot.

The first man came back in drunken heat, initiated by his and her glee.
No one else could beat his slow, deliberate means of creating ecstasy.
Man Number Two was attracted to her by this time
and didn't know what to do to change her mind.

The first guy and she were friends again for a month or
so until he found out another man had been knocking at her door.
She couldn't think straight or care
about ending a love affair.

In a bout of jealousy that she began,
she lost that first man.
She began to be inseparable from her second man friend
after accepting that her time with Number One had come to an end.

For half of the following year, after really caring deeply for the second guy,
she didn't shed a tear for the first guy and didn't even wonder why.
As she began to feel trapped and was frequently apart from her lover,
her resolve to be true to him was sapped and once again she was
forced to discover

that she had hidden her feelings for the first man by being with the
second guy.
She slowly began to understand the past six months had been a big lie
where she had covered up feeling after feeling of love for the first one.
Her deception needed to be undone.

Time wasn't on her side, for Number Two had to go away
and she couldn't split with him by his departure day.
She concentrated on loving the second guy with all of her heart
and tried to find the truth without tearing herself or someone else
apart.

By this time, she doubted her distant lover's feelings for her.
He convinced her that, one day soon, his wife she'd be.
Number One had been kind and gentle to her
after saying that his lover is all she could ever be.

He also began to distance himself from her soon after her fiancé
pulled away.
In every instance, it seemed the price of deception she'd pay.
One right after the other, she finally let both men go.
She should have done that a long time ago.

She feels empty, hurt, and confused.
She also feels like a user who was slightly used.
Now she knows the real pain
of love and doesn't want to ever feel it again. (Insane!)

They Both Deserved Each Other

There once was a young, heartbroken girl who'd experienced so
much pain
she decided it was useless to trust or love a man.
Even after she made this decision, she gave a few men the chance
to once again break her heart in the wild game of romance.

So she finally got the idea that her job in life was to lose
in every game of love she played because of the ruthless men she'd choose.
At one point in time, she was lucky enough to find
someone as sentimental and heartbroken as she, someone twice as kind.

They pretended to be sister and brother
until they found out that they really needed each other.
The guy lost contact with his loved fiancé
and experienced hurt in every way.

He was afraid of getting heartbroken again,
so he decided that his "sister" would be more than his friend,
For he knew that she was warm and loving, but vulnerable
and wouldn't put him down, for they would be inseparable.

After two weeks of talking to her, people began to tell him
that she was going out with someone else. This upset him
so much that he became angry at her and wouldn't speak,
for he began to think that she was what he didn't seek.

He wouldn't tell her of the many times she was nowhere to be found,
and she wouldn't tell him that she felt he was just messing around.

He didn't tell her that, for her, he sent his family home.
She didn't tell him that he brought back memories of the past that needed to be gone

forever from her mind, heart, and soul.
they failed to tell each other that their relationship was their lifetime goal.
As a result of this, they had a big misunderstanding
in which she failed to tell the kind of truth he was demanding.

He wanted to believe her, but the rumors weren't in her favor.
He wanted to continue their relationship, but the hurt he couldn't savor.
He said she made him feel like nothing
because of what had happened with his cousin

and because of the untrue rumors and innocent episodes he'd witnessed.
During the period of his decision-making, they both were distressed.
He was distressed because of the empty feeling she caused.
She was distressed because she needed him most of all.

She knew that their relationship would be one with security
because, together, they'd be happy eternally.
Their feelings they couldn't deny.
Their anguish was deep, deep on the inside,

and bitter tears she began to cry
because of all of the unhappiness caused by one lie,
because of the smoldering emotions she couldn't cover,
and because they both deserved each other.

Midnight Dream

One beautiful, starry, moonlit midnight, I had a dream
and in that dream, I became the victim of a man I'd never seen.
He kidnapped me over long miles of never-ending rough roads
to a place called Love Land, and what did I behold?

There was a gigantic marble palace in the midst of a garden
and beside the palace was a sparkling brook filled with clear, cold water.
There were so many sweet-smelling flowers and trees I almost
fainted,
then suddenly, as quick as lightning, my dream world became tainted.

In the middle of that paradise was the man who broke my heart,
the very same man who told me we would never part.
He promised me sweet happiness and love eternally.
All of these promises were broken, and I ached internally.

I pretended to be happy outwardly and always wore a smile.
My pain subsided after a long while.
Sometimes the thought of him made my eyes overflow with tears—
tears that were too bitter for a young lady of my years.

I knew that I would taste bitterness one day,
but the bitterness took years to go away.
As thoughts of the past coursed through my mind,
I looked into his eyes and decided to leave the past behind.

I walked over to him and explained the situation.
I asked for his help, and he needed no further explanation.
He took my hands in his and pulled me close to him
And said, "I love you, honey, and our future is no longer dim."

Exactly at that moment, I woke up from my dream
and looked out the window to where the beautiful stars could be seen.
Because I was half asleep, I heard a voice that only I could hear.
It said, "I'll be yours 'till death do us part', my sweet dear."

Memories of the Magic

I have memories of our first day, our first kiss,
the ecstasy we created that I'll always miss,
your sweet lovemaking, your tender caress,
the feel of your hands, oh, the tenderness,

the admiration and respect, the comments of flattery,
the interesting conversations, the uniqueness of chattering,
your arm around my shoulder, your warm hand in mine,
the look of satisfaction could only be erased by time.

On the other hand, I have memories of you walking away,
correcting my statements, not listening to what I had to say,
you turning in the other direction when I approached you,
you avoiding my eyes when you thought I loved you,

you being too busy when we needed to talk,
you running when you only had to walk,
your look of disgust when I came your way,
you acting like I clouded over a perfect, sunny day.

Most of all, I have memories of trying to forget your charming smile,
knowing all the time, it would take a very long while
traveling the long, lonely mile.

In Memory of You

A small ripple in the ocean
approximates the slight commotion
that your mercenary desires made,
but your lovemaking, her body craved.

She imagined all that you were holding back,
so she didn't feel like just another doormat.
She understands men like you
who do only what they have to do.

Lovemaking without love was a lot of fun with you,
so it never made her feel at all blue.
In memory of you, she has a new outlook,
a new desire, and a new book.

Because of you, she knows that she's okay
after the lovers who've come her way.
Maybe she's meant only to please
because it comes with such spontaneity and ease.

She'll be your love vessel in her mind
until the very end of her memory's time.

Just One Second

It took her so long to find that special one.
In just one second, he was gone,
and suddenly, she was all alone.

It took an eternity to build up respect and trust.
In just one second, it was all destroyed by lust,
and life had lost its meaningful thrust.

After months of wavering, he finally believed in her.
In just one second, she was shocked to incur
his feelings of contempt—intense and bitter.

After loving her for so very long,
he couldn't forgive her for that one wrong.
In just one second, he smiled and said, "So long."

What took months to build up, took one second to tear down.
When the lady finally comes around,
she'll realize that love is like a child's toy—
considerable time is required to create, but just one second can
destroy.

Mixed Up Men

You make women feel oh, so good,
commenting on their beauty and womanhood.
You tell them that there are too few men,
so some must be shared, and you say it again and again.

You make sweet love to them and show them ecstasy.
After it's over, you say you must be free.
You can't be honest no matter how hard you try
and always end up telling the gentle women goodbye.

You all have an extreme case of lost integrity,
and I guess this is the way it will always be.
All of your love affairs will turn into hate
unless you get yourselves together before it's too late.

How Can You?

How can you smile while I cry
because of what you did before saying goodbye?
How can you be happy while I'm so sad
as a result of the heartbreak I've had?

How can you go on and leave me behind
even though true success I may never find?
How can you hold someone else so very close
seeing the loneliness your ex-lover knows?

How can you be content while I remain restless
though you know this situation is really useless?
How can you stand up after making me fall
because I was the most serious of all?

How can you hold on to peace so dear
while my racking sobs are all I hear?
How can you pretend to have no one
when we know you're with someone?

How can you exaggerate frustration and contrition
like you're the one with the pleading petition?
How can you be so satisfied while I beg
and search for my spirit, which is certainly dead?

My heart is cold; my trust is gone.
Forever and ever, I'll be all alone.

The Helpful Someone

You soothed a lonely woman and gave her ecstasy,
and that young woman was none other than me.
Why was I so lonely? Why did I need love so bad?
Was it because of my weakness or the mistakes I made in the past?

To be truthful about the matter, I don't know the answers myself.
All that I know is that I needed someone else—
someone else to hold me, someone else to care,
someone to make me know happiness exists somewhere,

someone to give me affection, someone to hold me close,
someone to quench the desires of which only one person knows,
someone to help me grow, someone to give me life,
someone who'd erase all of the memories of past strife,

someone to make me happy, someone to hold my hand,
someone, anyone, who tried to understand.
All I needed was someone who showed interest in me,
and you were that someone who for one day gave me totality.

What Does It All Mean?

From two lonely people, what have we become?
Have we become serenity, or have we become a storm?
Both of us were players who made our own rules
and used our charm and intelligence as love's only tools.

So now we find ourselves trapped, unable to get loose
for fear that the wrong path is what we'll choose.
You won't open up your heart and let me in.
You won't disclose the key that will make me your special friend.

You won't let out the things that you hold inside.
Your past, you continue to hide.
My image of you is a figment of my imagination,
for my inquiries about the true you bring considerable indignation.

Importantly, you won't answer my questions about her child
so that I can decide if I should get lost for a long while.
I, too, kept my past locked deep on the inside
because of certain actions you would certainly deride.

I treated you wrong right in your face
and left scars only time can erase.
Because I love you, I made a lot of mistakes.
I forfeited my future, cast aside my pride,
and suffered many heartbreaks.

What does it all mean?
Did we do these things for the heck of it
or for the rich rewards of true love
that we haven't yet seen?

Illusions

You were supposed to be my first lover.
With you, the thrills of lovemaking I planned to discover.
Our plan was destroyed by a selfish man
who only believes in getting all he can.

I ran away from the realities of him and me,
heedless of the fact that this was my destiny.
I ran into worse troubles than I ran away from,
wondering about the young lady I've become.

Some of my friends misunderstand my life plan.
Only you know of the sweet person I really am.
I'm accused of doing things I'd never do,
and the only thing keeping my spirit alive is my love for you.

Even my love for you is causing me trouble,
for there seems to be doubt as to whether we love each other.
The lies you tell and the promises you brcak
do nothing more than put my confidence in you at stake.

Even if we stopped the many rumors that we hear,
the illusions still wouldn't disappear.

Men of Hypnotism

The first man of hypnotism made me cry,
so they soothed me with the softness of a sweet lullaby.
Next came one guardian angel of them all,
the loving protector who never let me fall.

Then came a man of hypnotism who was shy but supreme;
he was never heard, but was always seen.
The cutie was skilled at deceit.
His total disposition was anything but sweet.

The Latin Lover tried to play the field,
but his little game overflowed and spilled.
I'm afraid one man of hypnotism was as nice as could be.
Unfortunately, I didn't want him to want me.

The jiver should've been the Latin Lover's brother,
for they had so much in common with each other.
One man of hypnotism was one of a kind.
He was the only stone wall I was able to find.

The terrible man of hypnotism was a barrel of fun
until we ended what we had begun.
One man of hypnotism, after all, was so city slick
that he made me sick.

The disguiser had really changed,
for he acted like a trapped animal that'd become deranged.
The liar made me lose my trust in men;
therefore, he was guilty of an unforgivable sin.

The miracle man was too good to be true;
he made me do things no one else could make me do.
The robot was a pain in the side
because he managed to cover up his manly pride.

Except for the first three, all have contrived to blow my mind,
but these men of hypnotism will certainly find
that though they hypnotize me and break my heart into pieces so
fine,
I'm going to hold on to this sanity of mine.

My Gift

When I departed from you, I left you a legacy of love,
a token of the influences of below and above.
The cruel, twisted smile betrayed us both.
The wrinkled brow had already defied our oath.

The crude animal heart hammered out a discordant beat.
The erect breasts resembled those of an animal in heat.
The feet trampled down everything good.
The fleshy arms delivered a blow as hard as wood.

The swaying hips served to entice men,
while the bulging crotch said, "Let's do it again."
The clear, innocent eyes reflected charm.
The long, strong legs protected her from harm.

The hands performed every deed just right.
The soft, clear skin absorbed the purest sunlight.
The aching back had borne too many heavy loads.
The calloused feet had traveled numerous, dusty roads.

The shapely body belonged to a goddess on high,
but we still had to say goodbye.
I really want to know the reason why.

Together

When I'm with you or without you,
I'm seeking, discarding, and discovering;
however, one bad dream serves to haunt
my every hour (both sleeping and waking).

It's a dream of conquering a wild stallion
that throws even the best-trained rider,
refuses to eat anything but the wildest oats,
and disobeys every order and command.

It's a dream of manning a stream
that flows with destructive turbulence
and pressured force
that tear down rapidly bit by bit
the highest mountain.

It's a dream of a powerful wind
that destroys everything in its turbulent path
with such animated vigor
that the bees forget how to make honey,

the dog forgets its enemy, the cat,
and man himself forgets how to outmaneuver woman
when she attempts to seduce him.

It's a dream of you and me—
together for the first time, the last time,
the only time.

Set Apart

Touching his body, but not his mind
always leaves me a couple of long steps behind.
Catching up is simply out of the question,
for capturing his heart is an impossible situation.

Sharing our wants, needs, desires, and longings,
we're even willing to share our few precious belongings.
We're playing a game—of what, I don't know.
We're traveling roads, and I don't know where they go.

If we obey our minds, we're caught in a vise.
If we obey our hearts, everything is a surprise.
We're together as far as others can see,
yet we're set apart according to you and me.

Angel of the Early Morning Hours

Heartbreak, a disappointment so shatteringly bleak
that a lonely midnight walk provided the only relief,
was the initial phase that made me fly
accidentally into the arms of the unknown passerby.

My answer to his persistence was, "No! No! No!"
And our separate ways we both did go.
More heartbreak, more disappointment in the course of that year
made me accept the unknown passerby without inhibition or fear.

The film of dust that covered his heart
was the only obstacle great enough to keep us spiritually apart.
In all other ways we were together as one,
me, my mirror, my comfort, and my fun.

The tremendous honesty, the forehead caress
made the unknown passerby my only source of happiness.
Only, by this time he was no longer unknown,
for the seeds of familiarity had long been sown.

And above us, the threat of discovery towered
though he had become my angel of the early morning hours.

They Can't Change It

I'm 15 years old, and they say I'm too young
for you because you're 22. They say that I'm dumb
when compared to you because you've been around
long enough to realize the naiveté you've found.

The words I've said to you, and the feelings you've inspired
aren't the words and feelings of a 15-year-old child.
If both of us were 22,
would they say that I'm too different from you?

If both of us were 15,
would they say it's all a dream?
I believe that age is nothing but a little number
that has them all in a gigantic jumble.

They're so confused that they can't even see
that their nasty remarks have no effect on you and me.

Beneath the Surface

Deep within the dark, hollow recesses of her cavernous soul,
she utters a cry for all the world to behold.
The tears refuse to fall from her blackened, swollen eyes,
and the smooth, placid expression catches everyone by surprise.

Yet she is uttering an awe-inspiring cry
for all of the toasted honey of life that has passed her by.
While reaching for the scorching, flaming suns of desire,
she's only trapped her emotions on an empty, solitary bier,

Experienced the inflammation of absolute pleasure,
and lost her happiness as one big hidden treasure.

She Doesn't Have Good Taste, Huh?

You say that she has no taste,
that her beauty and education are going to waste
simply because she's with someone whom you could never pride.
Did you ever stop to think that maybe he's beautiful on the inside,

And that you're the one who has no taste
for letting one of nature's fine works of art go to waste?
Looks go only as far as the skin;
however, true beauty simply flows from within.

Don't criticize the young lady again,
for she's the lady who has a truly **beautiful** man.

To My Sweetheart at Christmas Time

Wishing you much happiness at this time of the year,
and hoping you'll be spending it with the one who's so dear.
Whenever the winds are blowing and you're chilled to the bone,
think of me, my love, and your thoughts will keep you warm.

Just sit by your Yuletide fire and dream sweet dreams of me
as you remember the present that I placed under your Christmas tree.

The Essence of Christmas Love

I look not for a gift from you to place under my Christmas tree,
for I know that your love for me isn't measured by your prosperity.
I feel no disappointment when I find out my arms
won't be filled with jewelry, trinkets, knickknacks, or charms.

I've discovered that the essence of true Christmas love really entails
immeasurable sacrifice and the unselfish giving of oneself without fail.

I Know Now

I know now what it means
to have unrealistic Christmas dreams.
I know now how it feels
to get shady Christmas deals.

I know now the familiar sounds
of the various Christmas get-downs.
I know now the mystical search
for the soft, gentle Christmas touch.

Foremost, however, I now know
of the bitter memories of Christmas long ago.

Christmas Blues

I feel so blue because I'm not with you,
the man of my dreams, my lover true.
I remember your touch, sweet and warm.
I remember the strength that protects me from harm.

I think of climbing mountains high and mighty
in order to reach you daily and nightly.
Christmas day seems empty and cold,
for you aren't here for me to behold.

Christmas night seems dark and bleak
and yields nothing that I want to seek.
The man I wish to hold, the man I wish to see
isn't here to share Christmas memories with me.

My Valentine

Some people called their spouse or mate on Valentine's Day,
and all of their past pain went away.
I couldn't call my Valentine on Valentine's Day.

We were separated by thousands of miles
that would have wiped away most people's smiles.
I knew that he thought of me that day even though he didn't call.
therefore, I smiled after all,

For he and I have loved one another through many years,
geographical changes, laughs, jokes, friends, and tears.
My Valentine is always on my mind
even on days other than Valentine's.

Mass Confusion

There's a love that can't be shown
because it shouldn't have grown
after the summer in which it was consummated.
The person who hides it has become exasperated.

She wants to tell the whole world how she feels.
She needs to tell the loved one about the sticky deals
that this one love affair is getting her into;
however, she can't hurt the one who loves her true.

She can't stop loving the man from the past
and can't get out of the lover's mold that she's cast.
She cries silently so that no one else knows
exactly why this forbidden love grows.

Soon the tale will come to light,
and still she'll be in a terrible plight.
Losing her mind, fighting against time,
she's guilty of an unforgivable crime.

The lady of love refuses to let go,
for she knows she'll get the man that she loves so.
Slipping, sliding, evading, and gliding into the pit of blackest night.
She's still convinced that she's perfectly right.

For Once

Why must life be so difficult for me
because I want to make a certain man happy?
This man, oh, if only he knew
that I think of him more than I see the morning dew.

Maybe he'd think of me as a woman instead of as a girl
who only knows the ways of the world,
a little girl who almost wrecked his life,
a little girl who's experienced lots of strife.

He told me to get lost, and I meekly obeyed.
Now how I wish I had stayed.
I loved him. I needed him. I wanted him so much,
but all that he could give me was his golden touch.

That, however, wasn't enough
because I really deserved the heavy stuff.
Patiently, I waited, watched, and grew
as he made up his mind about what he wanted to do.

Heartbroken and sad,
almost stark-raving mad,
I trampled on,
and then he was gone.

For once, why doesn't he come on back
and let us, together, make a sacred love pact?

Truth

On the surface, she's happy and cool.
Underneath, she's a persistent fool.
She's fooling everyone, including herself
because she longs for someone else.

She wants to be his joy, his pride
and wants desperately to stick by his side.
And who's this man she wants so bad,
this man who makes her joyful or sad?

He's none other than a lover from the past,
a relationship that couldn't possibly last.
Yet he wants to have no part of her.
He's afraid that she'll somehow stir

those old passions up some more.
He's afraid of another man she's supposed to adore.
She doesn't know how to let him know
about all of the things she's already let go,

about how she feels about him right now,
and about her insecurity of that eternal vow.
Thus, she's still unhappy and unsure,
depressed, disappointed, and very insecure

about that eternal flame
that's playing a hide-and-seek game.

And Still I Hope

What is it like to have yet not have,
to love yet not love,
to be loved yet not be loved?

Does it hurt to need and not be needed,
to want and not be wanted,
to desire and not be desired?

Would you like to create, then see it destroyed,
to find, then see it stolen,
to give, then see it given away?

As for me, I'd like to need and be needed,
to want and be wanted,
to desire and be desired.

Yet all that happens is my creations are destroyed,
my treasures are stolen,
and the beautiful love I give is given to someone else.

And still I hope—
that his eyes will be opened so that he can see,
that his hands will be touched so that he can feel,
and that his senses will be sharpened so that he can perceive.

And still I hope—
that his heart will pound with an expressive desire
designed especially to quench my blazing fire.

Only Tonight

When naught was left but life itself,
she still struggled to make her life the best.
For love, peaceful freedom, and dreams had been long lost,
and idle hopes were the main cause.

Hopes for success, prestige, and financial rewards
had made her throw away all of the wrong cards.
Now she's alone with no one in charge.
She has one last chance to make a new start.

Through it all, people hope she's learned
that real happiness comes from within
and that there are few things as good as true love from men.

Sweet, tender caresses and enjoyable evenings are okay,
but they don't mean a thing if they're only for tonight or today.
If tonight is the only time that she's beautiful and warm,
then she doesn't need his touch or his charm.

If tonight is the only time that he acknowledges her presence,
then she doesn't want his sweet effervescence.
If she's his only tonight
and not after morning light,

then something definitely isn't right,
and theirs is indeed a sad plight.

Sunlight

A burst of summer sunlight after eternal rain
helps her feel like she's once again sane.
Her sunlight, her Romeo true,
is none other than little old you.

The charming smile,
the winning style,
the pimp walk,
the polished talk

all combine to attract,
and that's a fact.
Though time is a limiting factor,
there are so many other stimulating effectors.

While their paths cross, they simply seek to enjoy
and keep the world from knowing that he's her summer toy.
He's hers to have and to hold until circumstances do them part;
until then, he's truly her heart.

Though tomorrow isn't theirs, they're thankful for today
and appreciative that sunlight does for a little while stay.

Fruited Dream

He's honest, gentle, lovable, and kind,
and his beautiful smile is one of a kind.
His walk so graceful and his skin so fair
remind her that a supernatural dwells there.

All is good, and all is sweet,
but there is, however, one defeat.
He can't be hers, and she can't be his,
and this mars the fruited dream of bliss.

This I Vow

Today I pledge my love, my heart
to this, our beautiful enriching start.
Your every wish, your every need,
I this day promise to try to heed.

Be it great or be it small,
I'll meet your expectations, some if not all.
I'll often be there when you're too weak
to attain the wondrous things you seek.

I might also be there when you're too strong
to let your heart's desires carry you along.
I can't promise that I'll always be there.
I can't promise that I'll always care.

But this I vow:
someday, some way, somehow
you'll realize that the depth of my feelings
isn't measured by lies' deceitful stealings.

Therefore, I won't promise you a flower bed,
but then I promise not eternal bloodshed.
I'll be realistic and just promise me,
and this is the way it'll always be.

And this I vow:
for me, you don't have to change your style,
for I appreciate your warmth, perception, gentleness, and smile

just the way they are.
This will take us long and far.
And until death do us part
you'll truly be my love, my heart.

Poisoning Pain

He promised her the truth
and the best years of his youth.
She was to be his wife,
for she was the essence of his life.

She really tried
until she discovered that he lied
about every single circumstance.
Now she wouldn't dare give him another chance.

She gave it her all,
and then she was ready to crawl
into a tiny little hole and die.
He dared to ask her why.

Insensitivity, callousness, ruthlessness—these are his assets,
so the rest of his traits you can certainly guess.
If she's supposed to hate him for the poisoning pain,
then something may be wrong with her brain.

She could never feel bitter for what he's done.
He did it because he's never had a loved one.
She could show him love, but she couldn't stop his hate.
She could respect and trust him, but he couldn't reciprocate.

She can believe in him ever
and let go of him never,
but she can't make it last
because of his deceitful past.

She can't play the part
of a forever-missing heart.
Thus, the poisoning pain
will forever remain
just as he'll always be the same.

Her Prince

When she wanted to be more than his friend,
it seemed that he had no time for her then.
But as one was multiplied by three,
it didn't matter that he wasn't free,

for he saw something that he hadn't seen before
and became a more frequent knocker at her door.
Now she doesn't know what to say or do
because she's afraid of how she stands with him too.

There's someone else to be considered,
so the matter really isn't trivial.
She knows what she's supposed to want,
but he and others don't.

That's why she's been confused ever since
he became the forbidden prince.

Memorable Mysteries

She remembers when you said you'd always be there.
She remembers when she thought you did really care,
but as time went on,
the beautiful feelings were gone.

For awhile, ecstasy dulled,
and the romance lulled.
Then she was fool enough to think you'd rekindled the fire
and that she was all you'd ever desire.

As usual, there was a but…
so your sacred alliance was fatally cut.
Slowly she began to unravel
the mysterious path your romance had traveled.

At first, she was hurt,
but then she became a second-time flirt
To cover up the pain time wouldn't erase
and to save her own little face.

Yes, it's over, with her once-sweet lover
and your feelings of contempt you don't have to cover.
She accepts the memorable mysteries both good and bad
even though she's the one who's been had.

One day when you're wise,
you'll wish you hadn't told so many lies.
You'll wish you'd loved her in the manner she deserved.
You'll wish your feelings hadn't swerved.

By then, it'll be too late
because she'll have someone who's greater than great.
It'll be love this time instead of a bitter man's hate.
Memorable yet mysterious,
next time it'll even be serious.

Sharing

He's yours, and he's mine.
He's limited, but that's fine.
You take the candy, and I'll take the cane.
We'll both be satisfied just the same.

You have what I may never possess,
but I don't need it anyway.
I have what you could never get,
but that's no regret.

You keep that; I'll keep this,
and sharing will become his most passionate kiss.

Expectations

Do you expect her to be true to you
when you sit at home doing what you want to do?
Should she expect you to be a total man
when away from reality you just ran?

You'd surely die from asphyxiation
if you sat and waited for your expectation,
And she'd die an early death
if she waited for your muscular wealth.

She'll love you from afar
and accept you as you are
as long as you understand
that she's looking for that real man.

Find yourself a faithful lover
who'll keep her urges under cover.
This way, you'll both be satisfied
because you at least tried

to measure up to the other person's expectations.
You're just victims of your individual aberrations.

The Inevitable Decision

When I see the smile on your face,
everything seems to fall in place.
I forget that you can never be in love with me
and that from your love's bondage, I'll never be free.

If all I can do is hold your hand,
then you still mean more to me than any other man
could possibly ever mean.
That's why I have to split the scene

and redirect my thoughts to the other guy
whose heart has already begun to cry.

Just a Sip

Give me a drink of cheap wine
and a morsel of bread on which to dine.
I'll be satisfied
as long as our love hasn't died.

I did it once; I'll do it again
as surely as I did it then.
All you have to say
is that you'll meet me halfway.

It's not as hard as you choose to make it.
I'm giving you love. How can you refuse to take it?
Maybe if I weren't available and free,
you'd desire to cherish me.

Since you can have what I possess,
I can't assuage your restlessness.
When it's too late, you'll want to love me.
I'll probably no longer be free.

Here's my final toast
to the man I love the most.

Her Mind's Photograph

She doesn't have a photograph of you,
but the one in her mind will do.
She sees you two engaging in light chatter
that isn't designed to impress or flatter.

She feels him lifting her gloomy mood
from one of despair to one that's good.
She hears her lilting voice softly caress him
to see if it can one day not possess him.

Within her web, he's slowly entrapped
until all of his resistance has been sapped.
Now he's no longer pursued,
for she becomes the one who's wooed

until she winds up in his bed.
Like one who's only first bled,
she's cautious and totally confused
and even feels a little used.

Time proves her to be wrong,
for they don't wait very long
before they're regular entertainment for the other
and he's become a gentler friend and lover.

She's surprised when she makes him smile;
he's surprised by her energetic guile.
Even though he's promiscuous and corrupt,
she can't seem to get enough.

It becomes time for them to say goodbye—
her body and soul still cry.

Just a Tear

You didn't give me a flower,
a necklace, or a fraction of an hour.
It appears that just a tear
separates me from happiness here.

Instead of thinking about the things you don't do,
I'll focus on the things I get from you.
Staying positive will go a long way
to make me love you and stay.

I look forward to a better life for you and me,
filled with celebration, laughter, and glee.
We'll change the tears to joyful smiles
that take us through our first and last miles.

He-Row

I didn't mean to cause her pain;
I wasn't just out for my own gain.
I simply wanted to enjoy his touch.
I hope I didn't ask too much.

I'm not the first, and I won't be the last,
so I'm not taking away his class.
He and I will take one day at a time
because we both know he'll never be mine.

Don't Try

Don't try to hide
your magnanimous pride.
Don't try to cover
the tracks of your latest lover.

Don't try to erase
the memory of her satisfied face.
Don't try to forget
you thought your relationship was a sure bet.

Don't try to decode
the maze-filled road.
Just try to comprehend
the reality of the end

of that sensuous dance
of your beautiful romance.

Passion

I can still see your beautiful smile
when you're not within a quarter of a mile.
Even though we were nothing more than lovers,
somehow something transcended the covers.

It was a contentment because we both learned
of the existence of something for which we yearned.
That something is hard to explain,
but it was devoid of anger, fury, and pain.

It was also devoid of love, a future, and promises broken,
yet it was much more than a skeletal token.
We asked nothing of each other beyond mutual satisfaction,
and that's what increased both of our attraction.

I touched you in many a beautiful way
that was more than just a romp in the hay.
I didn't ask for something you couldn't give;
I just wanted our passion, respect, and trust to live

one day at a time.
You hold a special place in this heart of mine.

The Ladies Man

Why did she dream about this suave guy
who's only made the women cry?
He'd never understand her insatiable greed
to live by a disreputable creed.

She'd never be able to comprehend
that he doesn't really mean to offend.
What's the purpose of her dream,
her desire for forbidden fruit, and her unheard scream?

Lady's Dream

I can't bear waiting for your call,
so I decide not to wait at all.
I decide that I'll go to sleep
so that your sweet memories I can keep.

While I'm sleeping, I have a dream
of an omnipresent thought, it seems.
I feel the warmth of your hand.
I see the smile whose presence I demand.

I detect the concern in your voice,
and I'm reminded of why you're my first choice.
Through the eyes of sleep, I'm complete,
for your protective love is all I meet.

See Sore, Sea Soar

Down, up, then down again,
it seems as if I just can't win.
I'd give you the world if I were able,
but that still wouldn't make our relationship stable.

What does she have that I don't have other than love from you?
Why can't I feel and do what I'm supposed to feel and do?
The riddle of these human emotions is still unsolved.
What you don't feel for me is still unresolved.

I hope you can hear the unheard voice.
I hope we both make the right choice.
I can't tell you the full story so you'll understand
why I'll never let you be *my* man.

He's Gone

Though he's with her in spirit, she's so alone
because her latest lover has truly gone.
When he comes back, she knows he'll say
that yesterday was the end of their day.

Regardless of the decision he makes,
the memorable occasions are all that it takes
to make everything worth her while.
She'll deposit this latest file

in the long stack that she's accumulated.
She refuses to be exasperated.
The tears have stopped flowing;
the light of hope has begun glowing.

As usual, she can't have what she really wants.
She has to get used to that fact
and straighten up her faulty act.

Forgotten

I wanted to tell you that everything was okay
and that I wouldn't bother you another day.
As usual, you wiped away my smile
and made me feel like a helpless child.

I don't know why you're afraid of me;
I don't know why the light you can't see.
When you decide on the true nature of you,
maybe you'll also decide what you should do

about the hypocrisy of Lady L.
All I can say is that time will tell.

The Truth

I could write honey-coated words
of starry nights or gentle snow-white birds.
I could tell you that I'll cross any ocean
and still any earthquake's motion

simply to be with you
doing what you want me to do.
I won't lie.
Let me tell you why.

If I speak the truth,
I'll tell you that through the hardships of youth
and the ravages of old age,
each day with you will be a potential page

of bad or of good.
I simply want to be your wife
and spend the rest of my life
exploring advantages and disadvantages of your manhood.

Means More to Me

If I can't do anything but kiss the tip of your nose,
it means more to me than a single white rose.
Every aspect of you makes me feel alive and whole.
You touch my very soul.

Misfortune

Fear grips my heart when I see you
and wonder what you'll possibly do
if I ask you out on yet another date.
Momentarily my heart is filled with both love and hate.

When the moment of fear has passed,
I feel tremendous love at last.
Don't ask me how. Don't ask me why.
Then I won't be forced to lie

about my feelings of love for you.
If I weren't in love with you, I wouldn't be feeling so blue.
My love is a terrible misfortune because you don't love me.
Soon the light I'll see,

and I'll be free
because my love for you will no longer control me.

My Baby

I can't talk to him in the middle of the day
because military duties took my baby away.
I cry softly in the middle of the night
because my baby isn't here to make everything all right.

I have many empty hours that can't be filled
because my baby's absence has already killed
the potential of a freshly plucked flower,
a warm embrace, or the millionth entertainment-filled hour.

I love him, need him, and miss him so much,
but my baby isn't here to give me just a touch
of his wide lips, perspiring musk-scented body, or strong hand.
I dare say that I understand

that my baby will come back day after tomorrow
and our reunion will be well worth today's sorrow.

I Miss You

I miss sitting on your lap eating,
trying to walk fast enough to keep up with you
after we've eaten an incredibly filling meal or two.

I miss the private war we engaged in quite frequently—
you waking me up an hour before I was ready to embrace the day,
the look of love in your eyes.

I miss trying to decide when we'll see one another at the end of the day,
wanting to be with you, yet not wanting to spend too much time,
loving you, but not wanting to be in love.

I miss lying beside you completely satisfied and happy
to relinquish control and let you satisfy me.
I miss seeing the relaxed expression of your satisfaction,
knowing that death could result from our mutual satisfaction.

I miss walking along holding your hand,
talking about one of the problems only the other can understand.
I miss apologizing to you for the millionth time
after committing for the millionth time the same crime.

I'm truly happy, for I'm finally in love
with you, a man who's happy to return my love.
I miss you right now, but more importantly than that
I humbly admit my love and respect, and that's a fact.

Dirty Laundry

In the middle of the week, we wash clothes.
It's only right now that my body knows
the binding love of together removing dirt
from our clothes. At this moment, I hurt

because I singularly trudge to the laundry room
feeling like a bride without her groom.
Your doing your laundry and I'm doing mine
indicate the independence that we've both mastered so fine.

We split the linen between the two of us
and don't let the ensuing laundry separation cause any fuss.
We may disagree about how to go to our laundry-washing ground,
but the one common facet we've both found

is a sense of transforming any minute, menial, trivial task
into a loving occasion beyond which neither of us can ask
the other person for anything more.
Our love is deep, and we shall love forevermore.

Major Decision

The sun is shining outside. It's such a beautiful day,
but I'm on the inside moping the time away.
I have to make a decision that will affect the rest of my life.
I have to decide if I can take a chance and become his wife.

He's fine when it comes to dinner, drinks, gifts, and sex,
but when it comes to the real test of love it seems that he forgets
to be warm, loving, gentle, and kind.
In fact, he seems not to be able to find

any quality time for the woman in his life
when he's faced with a major decision or strife.
Part of me says leave him alone
and after awhile the memories of him will be gone.

That part of me says, "Don't let history repeat itself."
The simple truth is that I can think of nothing else
but the warm love we used to share
and the time we spent together, going everywhere,

doing so much, and enjoying every hour.
Now our love seems like a dying flower.
The other part of me says hold on to him at all cost,
but I feel like the battle has already been lost.

He acts like he doesn't care and hates my guts.
I still love him so very much.
I love him enough to give him up if I have to.
For him, I'll do whatever I must do.

He's worried about the monsters he's been able to create.
I truly hope that it's not too late,
for I really don't want our love to end.
I just want to continue to be his friend.

Anything else will leave me bitter and sore
because I want to be his forevermore.

African Prince

For many years, I've loved you and wanted you so much,
and now I have the chance to enjoy more than just your touch.
After waiting so long, you'd think I'd be afraid
to risk losing you just for the sake of getting laid

by someone else's man who's another person's housemate;
however, I don't understand myself of late.
I used to be sensitive, loving, and slow to hate.

But now I'm selfish, passionate, and carefree.
Please be patient while I unravel the mysteries of me.
Understand that I still love you deeply,

my African prince,
and I'll soon end these incidents.

Wait, Wait, Wait

How do I stop the pain
that turns sunshine into rain?
Do I dare go to him
and tell him of my latest whim?

Is my other friend just playing a game
to disassociate me from his name?
Is he hiding his feelings of caring
and pretending the moments we're sharing

are just occasions of mutual pleasure
that neither of us can treasure?
I know I love my other friend
to no end.

He's afraid, and I'm afraid
of the trap that could be laid
if I love him and he loves me.
I just have to wait and see.

Our World

Did either of them ever love me
enough to die for me?
Did either of them ever love me
enough to cry for me?

Could they ever love me
enough to grow with me?
Could they ever love me
enough to go with me

beyond the realms of the physical world
into a world where only the two of us exist?
Our bodies, minds, and souls would intertwine with such joy
that we would be happier than a child
playing with his or her first toy.

In our world, we would be completely happy and free.
I await the day when my man will enter this private world with me.

My Man

There are others that I could love, other hearts that I could touch,
but my heart is only set on one man. I love him so much.
There are some who are stronger, richer, and more likely to succeed,
but the only man I want is the one man I need.

There are men who are more ambitious or more self-sufficient,
but I'm only interested in one man who's ever so efficient.
There are men who are more suave or more full of cheer,
but I only want to deal with one man who's so dear.

Some may think that there are better men because of the decrees
of destiny,
but the best man of all is the one I love, who also deeply loves me.

Your Touch

Gentle as a summer breeze, sweet as a rose,
you touched me from my head to my toes.
A mental touch, a spiritual touch, it meant so much,
for it marked the termination of a long, treacherous search.

Your touch was the beginning of something good,
for it was the final step toward true womanhood.
My darling, my dear, I'll forever be indebted to you
for that wonderful touch from you, my lover true.

If, If, If

If you can forget the women of the past,
if you can start a relationship that will last,
then confusion and strife will disappear,
and you'll know love is at last here.

If you can be yourself for just a little while,
if you can consider the implications behind my smile,
then you and I can get along,
and I'll forget the times you treated me wrong.

If you can accept my love for what it is,
if you can strive for success and eternal bliss,
then you can be the man who's right for me,
and you'll erase all of the past disparity.

If, if, if you could just be mine,
then I'm sure you'd grow to love me in due time.
First you have to make me your number one,
and then we can plan the beautiful moments to come.

Love and Hope

No one knows the taste of love
unless she has truly loved.
No one knows the promise of hope
unless she has been in the shadow.

I sit alone tonight basking in the glow of knowledge,
for I have been in love so long and deep
that time stood still
and I did not know hunger, pain, fear, or insecurity.

I have also known the fruit of a hope
that helped me to put one foot in front of the other
so that I could proceed toward
the light of your love.

My darling, my dear, I have come to terms
with the fact that our love is the deepest
and no other can give me love or hope.
I hope to always love you.

What Is Love?

What is love besides a sweet word
that I've time after time whispered and heard?
Was it love that made me feel like a child
and wiped away my beautiful smile?

Was it love that made me patient and kind
in spite of the callous indifference that I didn't want to find?
Is it love that makes her try to hold on to you
like a confused child who doesn't know what she should do?

Is it love that keeps others from letting you go?
Does love make me believe your story when I don't know
what kind of force drives you to satisfy us all?
Will love be the ultimate downfall

of this madness that's consuming you and me
and letting us know that we'll never be free?

Love Is....

People say that love is undefined and no one knows its measure.
To me, darling, you are love, its bittersweet, golden treasure.
Love is that beautiful smile that only you can give.
Love is the kind of life that only we can live.

Love is that salty tear that you create, then swiftly wipe away,
the touch of your hand, gentle and warm, the burst of a new day.
Yes, darling, I love you for the above reasons and many more.
I'll continue to love you today, tomorrow, forevermore.

About the Author

Dr. Linda Amos started writing poems as a teenager then began writing essays and short stories a couple of years later. Linda's written poems that encourage, share, and explain. Her poems are about subjects such as communication, growth, courage, love, and compromise.

Linda is a member of Zeta Phi Beta Sorority, Inc. She's received many academic, sorority, and workplace awards while honing her writing skills. Linda has enjoyed a successful corporate career in which she strengthened her writing skills working in the chemical and pharmaceutical industries as a research chemist, science catalog writer, science writer, and medical writer.

Linda has a B.S. degree in chemistry from Tougaloo College in Tougaloo, MS and M.A. and Ph.D. degrees in chemistry from Princeton University in Princeton, NJ. When she's not writing, Linda enjoys reading about investments, nutrition, and health; cooking healthy food; and talking with family and friends, especially while walking.

Coming Soon

Beautiful Love Poems

Courage Motivational Poems

Growth Motivational Poems

Success Motivational Poems